BADASS
AFFIRMATIONS
the Coloring Book

Also by Becca Anderson

Badass Affirmations

Badass Affirmations Habit Tracker

Badass Advice

Positively Badass

The Book of Awesome Women

The Book of Awesome Black Women

Female, Gifted, and Black

The Book of Awesome Girls

The Book of Awesome Woman Writers

You Are an Awesome Woman

The Joy of Self-Care

BADASS
AFFIRMATIONS
the Coloring Book

**Motivational Coloring Pages & Positive
Affirmations for Your Inner Badass**

BECCA ANDERSON

mango
PUBLISHING

CORAL GABLES

Cover & Interior Design: Megan Werner

Cover Illustration: moremar / stock.adobe.com

Interior Illustrations: aigann25, Creative Juice, Dariia, Felizebeth, Galakam, ioanna_alexa, iStarDesign, Knstart Studio, KozyPlace, Maksim, mar_mite_, Nadezda Grapes, Olga, Olly Kava, Yelyzaveta, Анастасия Гевко, Екатерина Анисимова / stock.adobe.com

For permission requests, please contact the publisher at:

Mango Publishing Group

2850 S Douglas Road, 2nd Floor

Coral Gables, FL 33134 USA

info@mango.bz

For special orders, quantity sales, course adoptions and corporate sales, please email the publisher at sales@mango.bz. For trade and wholesale sales, please contact Ingram Publisher Services at customer.service@ingramcontent.com or +1.800.509.4887.

Badass Affirmations the Coloring Book: Motivational Coloring Pages & Positive Affirmations for Your Inner Badass

ISBN: (pb) 978-1-68481-291-2 (hc) 978-1-68481-292-9

BISAC category code: GAM019000, GAMES & ACTIVITIES / Coloring Books

WELCOME!

The book you hold in your hands is what you make of it. Some use coloring books as art therapy to release some stress, some as a hobby to pass the time. Based on my internationally bestselling book *Badass Affirmations*, this coloring book can offer you a little something extra. Since I love coloring as a relaxing activity, plus I am a huge believer in affirmations to stay inspired, I decided to combine the two into a coloring book!

Filled with positive affirmations, my goal is to help you meditate on the words while you color, so they really sink in. But wait, let's first clarify what affirmations are all about.

Affirmations are positive statements that you make out loud, every day, to help you shift your mindset in a positive and productive way. These statements can be about literally anything. For example, if you are trying to increase your self-confidence, you could say something like, "I am proud of myself." Or if, let's say, you just had a bad breakup and you're trying to shift your focus from your dating life (or lack thereof) to your career—then you could say to yourself, "I am valued, and everyone loves to work with me." It's all about what changes you want to make—how you want to improve your mindset and, ultimately, your life.

Now, one of the main benefits of affirmations is that they help you to change how you think over time. You won't wake up one morning, say to yourself that you're going to be happy from now on, and then have the best day of your life every day until you die. (Well, you probably won't, anyway—I suppose anything is possible.) But if you commit to taking five minutes of your day to tell yourself that you are a beautiful, capable person who will achieve all you are working for, you'll find that after a couple of weeks, you're actually starting to believe yourself.

Maybe you'll stop cringing every time you say them, or maybe you'll start to notice all of the small steps you're making toward your big goals—the steps that have been made easier now that you know, and I mean really know, that you're capable of anything you set your mind to.

THE ART OF SELF-AFFIRMATION:

How to Use This Book

Let the affirmations sink in as you color these pages. Feel free to go from start to finish, or pick up the book, randomly open to an affirmation, and let those words be your guiding thought for the day. If you are *really* resonating with this power-thought, keep using it every day and let it become your mantra.

Use these inspired ideas in speeches, on your bulletin board, in your email signature, as your Twitter handle, or on your social media. Hey, if it is your favorite ever Big Thought, get a tattoo on your inner wrist where you see it all the time and are reminded of your personal worth and of the great big, beautiful world we all live in.

Read a few and really "power up" for your day—sort of like getting a booster shot in word form. If you are getting ready to do a presentation, a sales pitch, an interview for your dream job, your next YouTube content, or any very important date, this affirmation can be the wind in your sails.

Chapter One

BADASS
SELF-CONCEPT

~~~~~~

Magic lies in challenging what seems impossible.

—Carol Moseley-Braun, the first female African American
elected to the United States Senate

I am unstoppable.

*I grow stronger after
every setback.*

I am on the right path.

~~~~~

**Character isn't inherited. One builds it daily
by the way one thinks and acts, thought by
thought, action by action. If one lets fear or
hate or anger take possession of the mind,
they become self-forged chains.**

—Helen Gahagan Douglas, whose political career took off
after the Great Depression, when she decided to leave
acting to work with the Democratic Party

I stay winning.

I am unfazed by people who doubt me.

I am my biggest supporter.

~~~~~

Do what you are afraid to do.

—Mary Emerson, author and philosopher whose love of deep conversation encouraged many of her friends, family members, and readers

I have my back.

I trust myself.

I cherish myself.

~~~~

Devote today to something so daring even you can't believe you're doing it.

—Oprah Winfrey, philanthropist and media titan whose various productions entertain and inform people worldwide

I create my own path.

I am comfortable achieving what I deserve.

I am an extraordinary person.

~~~

Never limit yourself because of others' limited imagination; never limit others because of your own limited imagination.

—Mae Jemison, first female African American in space; her role as a science specialist led her to conduct motion-sickness and weightlessness experiments on herself and her fellow astronauts

I can do what has never
been done before.

I am unlimited.

I fight for my beliefs.

~~~

Leave your home, O youth,
and seek out alien shores.
A wider range of life has been ordained for you.

—Petronius, "Director of Elegance" for Emperor Nero's court,
where he decided on matters of taste and style, and reputed
author of the *Satyricon*

I'm the creator of my own life experience.

I'm sure of myself.

I have my back.

~~~~~

I will not be vanquished.

—Rose Kennedy, matriarch of a family made up partially of politicians; she was their anchor and assisted in many of their political (and personal!) victories

I respect myself and my needs.

I always know my worth.

I am 100 percent committed to myself.

~~~~~

We are not interested in the possibilities of defeat. They do not exist.

—Queen Victoria of England and Britain's second-longest reigning monarch (outlasted only by Queen Elizabeth II), who spearheaded England's Victorian Era with her stringent personality, morals, and ethics

I feel safe and confident to be my authentic self wherever I go.

I am the main character.

I got this.

~~~~~

Hope begins in the dark, the stubborn hope that if you just show up and try to do the right thing, the dawn will come. You wait and watch and work: you don't give up.

—Anne Lamott, author of novels and nonfiction works focused on family and real (or realistic, in the case of her fiction) people

Chapter Two

BADASS SELF LOVE

~~~

Beauty is when you can appreciate yourself. When you love yourself, that's when you're most beautiful.

—Zoë Kravitz, who broke out of the shadow of her parents' music and acting success to garner her own in *X-Men: First Class* and *Fantastic Beasts: The Crimes of Grindelwald*

I love taking care of myself, and I love being taken care of.

I am focused on myself.

I am always showing appreciation to my body.

~~~~~

Being sexy is all about attitude, not body type. It's a state of mind.

—Ameesha Patel, winner of awards in both economics and acting, whose overnight acting success led her to leave finance behind in favor of her very successful career in film

I am beautiful on the inside and outside.

I am comfortable with myself.

I think of myself as sexy.

〜〜〜

To dance confident in fringe panties when you're five-four with cellulite is a great thing.

—Drew Barrymore, who overcame addiction and a wild reputation to garner amazing success as an actress, producer, and model

I feel good about myself.

I am comfortable in my own skin.

When I look in the mirror, I see beauty.

~~~

I see myself as sexy. If you are comfortable with it, it can be very classy and appealing.

—Aaliyah, singer and actress who started her career at the age of twelve; her life was cut short by a plane crash only ten years later

I am comfortable
in my clothes.

I am naturally beautiful.

I recognize that I
have true beauty.

～～～

*Imperfection is beauty, madness is genius
and it's better to be absolutely ridiculous
than absolutely boring.*

—Marilyn Monroe, who took advantage of a chance
discovery by a photographer to change her life and build a
successful modeling and acting career

I am naturally magnetic.

I possess inner beauty.

I am original

~~~

Beauty has so many forms, and I think the most beautiful thing is confidence and loving yourself.

—Kiesza, who worked as a code breaker in the Royal Canadian Navy before competing in Miss Universe Canada and then moving on to become a singer-songwriter

I am whole.

I am worthy of all good things.

I am loving, lovable, and loved.

~~~~~

The first and worst of all frauds is to cheat one's self. All sin is easy after that.

—Pearl Bailey, United Nations advisor who started out as a Tony Award-winning Broadway actress and singer

I am so special and rare.

I am magnetic.

I am the prize.

~~~~

**Just don't give up trying to do what you really want
to do. Where there is love and inspiration,
I don't think you can go wrong.**

—Ella Fitzgerald, the first female African American Grammy
Award winner; her incredible jazz singing went on to win her
a total of twenty-one Grammys

I am incomparable.

My beauty within and without are equal.

I am a queen and I act like it

~~~~~

Elegance is the only beauty that never fades.

—Audrey Hepburn, the *Breakfast at Tiffany*'s star who's won every major kind of acting award, not to mention the Presidential Medal of Freedom

Chapter Three

BADASS AT WORK

～～～

It's never too late to be what you might have been.

—George Eliot, also known as Mary Ann Evans, who
subedited for *The Westminster Review* and was known for
her novels' exploration of human psychology

I belong in a position of power.

Abundance is my birthright.

I inspire others to succeed.

~~~

All things are possible until they are proved impossible—and even the impossible may only be so, as of now.

—Pearl Buck, humanitarian and Pulitzer Prize-winning author who was the first female American Nobel laureate, winning the Nobel Prize for Literature

People trust my opinions and expertise.

Everyone wants to work with me.

I am a good decision maker.

~~~~~

If you want to stand out, don't be different, be outstanding.

—Meredith West, esteemed professor whose research interests include how behavior develops in humans and animals

Nothing is impossible for me.

I am respected and valued.

Everyone values my opinions and ideas.

~~~~~

If you want something in life, you have to go out and get it, because it's just not going to come over and kiss you on your lips.

—Renee Scroggins, member of the band ESG, which she started with her sisters and a couple of friends, under the supervision of her mother, before any of them graduated high school

My actions speak louder than my words.

I am unstoppable.

I make my dreams a reality.

〰️

If one is going to change things, one has to make a fuss and catch the eye of the world.

—Elizabeth Janeway, author whose highly praised psychological insight and incredible writing led to her being known as a modern Jane Austen

My discipline is stronger than my motivation.

I am living a life of my own design.

Everyone wants to work with me.

~~~

Think bigger! Be a millionaire, don't marry one.

—Nell Merlino, the 2000 Forbes Trailblazer who created "Make Mine a Million Business" and "Take Our Daughters to Work Day"

I use my success to help others.

I build my coworkers
up as I grow.

I leave no one behind.

~~~~

If it's a good idea...go ahead and do it. It is much easier to apologize than it is to get permission.

—Grace Murray Hopper, programmer who joined the US Navy during WWII and who later headed the team that made the first computer language compiler; without her work, modern computer programming would not be possible

My actions speak louder than my words.

I make myself proud.

I am good at my job.

~~~

I was the conductor of the Underground Railroad for eight years, and I can say what most conductors can't say—I never ran my train off the track and I never lost a passenger.

—Harriet Tubman, who led hundreds of enslaved Americans to freedom before working as, among other jobs, a Union spy during the Civil War

I am always generating more business.

I attract the highest quality clients.

Everything I touch turns to gold.

~~~~~

The beaten track does not lead to new pastures.

—Indira Gandhi, who rose to political popularity through her work to revitalize farming; she later became India's third prime minister

Chapter Four

BADASS AT RELATIONSHIPS

～～～

To friendship every burden's light.

—Aesop

I am always making new friends everywhere I go.

I am encouraging and supportive of others.

I am kind to myself and others.

～～～

"If you're brave enough to say goodbye, life will reward you with a new hello."

—Paulo Coelho, author of the mystical international bestseller *The Alchemist*

I am forgiving and nonjudgmental.

I am open to learning new perspectives.

I listen carefully to deeply understand others.

～～～

I love family, my children...but inside myself is a place where I live all alone and that's where you renew your springs that never dry up.

—Pearl S. Buck, humanitarian and Pulitzer Prize-winning author who was the first female American Nobel laureate, winning the Nobel Prize for Literature

I never compare myself to others.

I am happy to compliment people.

I am appreciative of everyone's unique qualities and my own.

~~~~~

Real friends are the ones you can count on no matter what. The ones who go into the forest to find you and bring you home. And real friends never have to tell you that they're your friends.

—Morgan Matson, bestselling American novelist

I feel safe and confident communicating my needs.

I only do what I feel comfortable doing.

I am confident upholding my boundaries.

~~~~

"She is a friend of my mind. She gather me, man. The pieces I am, she gather them and give them back to me in all the right order."

–Toni Morrison, author of the classic *Beloved*

I treat others with love and respect because that is how I treat myself.

I am encouraging of my dreams and other people's.

I love myself the way I love my best friends.

～～～

To us, family means putting your arms around each other and being there.

—Barbara Bush, First Lady from 1988 to 1992; her son Neil's dyslexia inspired her to champion literacy issues, and she founded the Barbara Bush Foundation for Family Literacy in 1989

I protect my peace.

I feel at ease taking me time when I need it.

I always stand up for my needs and ideas.

~~~

I believe that the greatest gift you can give your family and the world is a healthy you.

—Joyce Meyer, author, TV host, radio host, and president of Joyce Meyer Ministries, a religious multimedia nonprofit

I wish good upon the world,
and it wishes good upon me.

I mind my own business.

I am free from the good
and bad opinions of others.

~~~

Two things you will never have to chase:
True friends and true love.

—Mandy Hale, bestselling author and starter of the Single
Woman movement encouraging women how to embrace
being single

I am not attached to how
things should be.
I let situations, people,
and myself flow freely.

I release the need
to judge or criticize.

Everything is always
working out for me.

~~~~~

Friendships between women, as any woman will
tell you, are built of a thousand small kindnesses...
swapped back and forth and over again.

—Michelle Obama, First Lady of the United States,
author of *Becoming*

Chapter Five

BADASS CONFIDENCE

~~~~~

It requires philosophy and heroism to rise above the opinion of the wise men of all nations and races.

—Elizabeth Cady Stanton, abolitionist and leader of the women's rights movement who helped organize the National Women's Suffrage Association and penned the revolutionary "Declaration of Sentiments"

I am capable.

I am a leader.

I go after what I want.

~~~~~

I came out of the womb a diva. All it means is you know your worth as a woman.

—Cyndi Lauper, singer, songwriter, and actress

I am successful

I am worthy.

I respect myself.

～～～

Some people say I'm attractive. I say I agree.

—Cybill Shepherd, actress and the winner of three Golden Globe awards; she began singing at the age of five and hasn't let anyone or anything stop her since

I am beautiful.

I am attractive.

I love myself.

~~~~~

Walking with a friend in the dark is better than walking alone in the light.

—Helen Keller

I will succeed.

I believe in myself.

*I achieve whatever
I put my mind to.*

~~~

**You can cry, but don't let it stop you. Don't cry
in one spot—cry as you continue to move.**

—Kina, famous YouTuber, singer, and songwriter who won
the "Doritos Crash the Super Bowl" musical competition

I can do anything.

I speak my mind.

I am intelligent.

~~~~~

**It is not easy to find happiness in ourselves,
and it is not possible to find it elsewhere.**

—Agnes Repplier, essayist and biographer with a sixty-five-year writing career; she had so much trouble learning how to read from her mother that, when she was ten, she finally taught herself

Every step I take is a step in the right direction.

I will learn from any failures and push forward.

I am changing the world.

~~~

It's a good thing to have all the props pulled out from under us occasionally. It gives us some sense of what is rock under our feet, and what is sand.

—Madeleine L'Engle, author and poet whose award-winning children's books encourage individuality and bravery

I can survive even my greatest fears.

I have important things to say.

I face my fears bravely.

~~~~~

If you always do what interests you, at least one person is pleased.

—Katharine Hepburn, acting legend and four-time winner of the Academy Award for Best Actress

I believe in myself.

I see myself as confident and successful.

I am transforming into a confident, beautiful person.

~~~~~

Revolution begins with the self, in the self.

—Toni Cade Bambara, award-winning author and director of the Theater of the Black Experience

About Becca Anderson

Becca Anderson is an author, teacher and writing instructor living in the San Francisco Bay Area. Originally from Ohio, Becca's background in women's studies has given her a lifelong passion for empowering women through their own herstory. The author of *The Book of Awesome Women*, Becca Anderson credits her first grade teacher as a great inspiration and runs several popular classes and workshops including "How to Put Your Passion on Paper."

Mango Publishing, established in 2014, publishes an eclectic list of books by diverse authors—both new and established voices—on topics ranging from business, personal growth, women's empowerment, LGBTQ studies, health, and spirituality to history, popular culture, time management, decluttering, lifestyle, mental wellness, aging, and sustainable living. We were named 2019 *and* 2020's #1 fastest growing independent publisher by *Publishers Weekly.* Our success is driven by our main goal, which is to publish high-quality books that will entertain readers as well as make a positive difference in their lives.

Our readers are our most important resource; we value your input, suggestions, and ideas. We'd love to hear from you—after all, we are publishing books for you!

Please stay in touch with us and follow us at:

Facebook: Mango Publishing

Twitter: @MangoPublishing

Instagram: @MangoPublishing

LinkedIn: Mango Publishing

Pinterest: Mango Publishing

Newsletter: mangopublishinggroup.com/newsletter

Join us on Mango's journey to reinvent publishing, one book at a time.

Printed in the USA
CPSIA information can be obtained
at www.ICGtesting.com
JSHW071730221023
50628JS00003BA/5